WILDLIFE SANCTUARIES

Ontario Ecoregions

- Coastal Hudson Bay Lowland
- Northern Lakes and Forests
- Lake Erie Lowland
- Eastern Great Lakes and Hudson Lowlands
- Hudson Bay and James Bay Lowlands
- Algonquin/Southern Laurentians
- Abitibi Plains and Riviere Rupert Plateau
- Lake Nipigon and Lac Seul Upland
- Hayes River Upland and Big Trout Lake

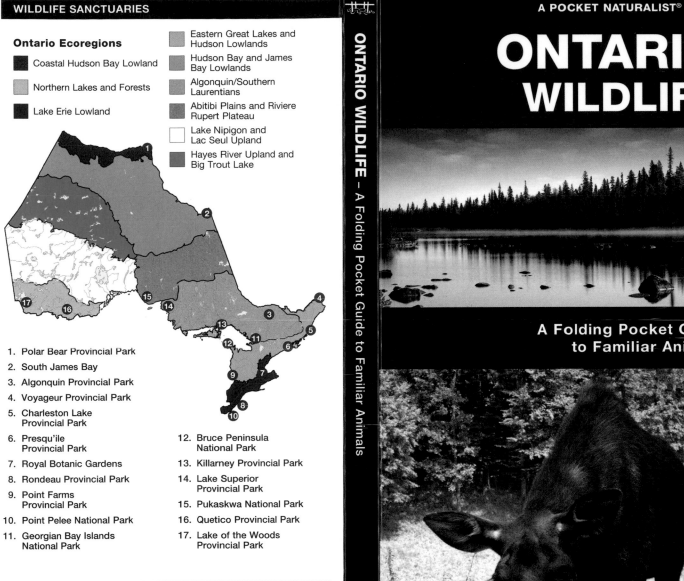

1. Polar Bear Provincial Park
2. South James Bay
3. Algonquin Provincial Park
4. Voyageur Provincial Park
5. Charleston Lake Provincial Park
6. Presqu'ile Provincial Park
7. Royal Botanic Gardens
8. Rondeau Provincial Park
9. Point Farms Provincial Park
10. Point Pelee National Park
11. Georgian Bay Islands National Park
12. Bruce Peninsula National Park
13. Killarney Provincial Park
14. Lake Superior Provincial Park
15. Pukaskwa National Park
16. Quetico Provincial Park
17. Lake of the Woods Provincial Park

Most illustrations show the adult male in breeding coloration. Colors and markings may be duller or absent during different seasons. The measurements denote the length of animals from nose/bill to tail tip. Butterfly measurements denote wingspan. Illustrations are not to scale.

Waterford Press publishes reference guides to nature observation, outdoor recreation and survival skills. Product information is featured on the website:
www.waterfordpress.com

 To order or for information on custom published products please call 800-434-2555 or email orderdesk@waterfordpress.com. For permissions or to share comments email editor@waterfordpress.com. 217126

ISBN 978-1-58355-283-4 $7.95 U.S.
UPC
10 9 8 7 6 5 4 3 2 1 Made in the USA

ONTARIO WILDLIFE – A Folding Pocket Guide to Familiar Animals

Kavanagh/Leung

A POCKET NATURALIST® GUIDE

ONTARIO WILDLIFE

A Folding Pocket Guide to Familiar Animals

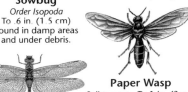

INVERTEBRATES

Earthworm
Lumbricus terrestris
To 10 in. (25 cm)

Sowbug
Order Isopoda
To .6 in. (1.5 cm)
Found in damp areas and under debris.

Common Snail
Haplotrema sportella
To 1 in. (3 cm)

Pond Leech
Macrobdella spp.
To 10 in. (25 cm)
Body has a line of red or black spots along the sides.

Green Darner
Anax junius
To 3 in. (8 cm)
Has a bright green thorax and a blue body. Rests with its wings open.

Paper Wasp
Polistes spp. To 1 in. (3 cm)
Told by slender profile and dark, pale-banded abdomen. Builds papery hanging nests.

Bumble Bee
Bombus spp.
To 1 in. (3 cm)
Stout, furry bee is large and noisy.

Mayfly
Order Ephemeroptera
To 1.25 in. (3.2 cm)
Has triangular wings and long "tails."

Monarch
Danaus plexippus To 4 in. (10 cm)
Note rows of white spots on edges of wings. Millions migrate between the US and the forests of central Mexico each year.

Fruit Fly
Drosophila melanogaster
To .1 in. (.3 cm)
Tiny fly is found near fermenting and rotting fruit.

Ground Beetle
Family Carabidae
To 1.5 in. (4 cm)
Glossy purple-green insect.

Cabbage White
Pieris rapae
To 2 in. (5 cm)
One of the most common butterflies.

Daddy Longlegs
Leiobunum vittatum
To .5 in. (1.3 cm)
Distinguished by small body and stilt-like legs.

Ladybug Beetle
Family Coccinellidae
To .5 in. (1.3 cm)
Red wing covers are black-spotted.

House Fly
Musca domestica
To .25 in. (.6 cm)
Has pale sides and light stripes down back.

Garden Spider
Family Araneidae
To 1.25 in. (3.2 cm)
White-spotted dark spider.

Silverfish
Lepisma saccharina
To .5 in. (1.3 cm)
Tapered insect is distinguished by its triple tail.

FISHES

White Sucker
Catostomus commersonii
To 30 in. (75 cm)
Has downturned, sucker-like mouth.

Lake Whitefish
Coregonus clupeaformis To 30 in. (75 cm)
Note concave forehead.

Lake Trout
Salvelinus namaycush To 4 ft. (1.2 m)
Dark fish is covered in light spots. Tail is deeply forked.

Lake Herring (Cisco)
Coregonus artedi To 21 in. (53 cm)

Rainbow Trout
Oncorhynchus mykiss To 44 in. (1.1 m)
Note reddish side stripe.

Brown Trout
Salmo trutta To 40 in. (1 m)
Has red and black spots on its body.

Brook Trout
Salvelinus fontinalis To 28 in. (70 cm)
Reddish side spots have blue halos.

Smallmouth Bass
Micropterus dolomieu To 27 in. (68 cm)
Jaw joint is beneath the eye.

Largemouth Bass
Micropterus salmoides To 40 in. (1 m)
Jaw joint extends beyond the eye.

Walleye
Sander vitreus To 40 in. (1 m)
Note white spot on lower lobe of tail.

Northern Pike
Esox lucius To 53 in. (1.4 m)
Note large head and posterior dorsal fin.

Pumpkinseed
Lepomis gibbosus To 16 in. (40 cm)
Green-orange fish has red-black spot on ear flap.

Brown Bullhead
Ameiurus nebulosus To 20 in. (50 cm)
Brown above, white below with mottled sides.

Yellow Perch
Perca flavescens To 16 in. (40 cm)
Note 6–9 dark "saddles" down its side.

Burbot
Lota lota To 3 ft. (90 cm)
Slender fish has a single chin barbel.

REPTILES & AMPHIBIANS

Wood Turtle
Glyptemys insculpta To 9 in. (23 cm)
Note sculpted shell and red-orange legs.

Spotted Turtle
Clemmys guttata To 5 in. (13 cm)
Dark shell is yellow-spotted.

Snapping Turtle
Chelydra serpentina
To 18 in. (45 cm)
Note knobby shell and long tail.

Painted Turtle
Chrysemys picta To 10 in. (25 cm)
Note red marks on outer edge of shell.

Red-eared Slider
Trachemys scripta To 11 in. (28 cm)
Common pet store turtle is often released in the wild.

Five-lined Skink
Plestiodon fasciatus
To 8 in. (20 cm)
Has 5 light dorsal stripes.

Common Garter Snake
Thamnophis sirtalis To 4 ft. (1.2 m)
Brownish snake has yellowish back stripes.

Smooth Green Snake
Opheodrys vernalis
To 26 in. (65 cm)

Eastern Hognose Snake
Heterodon platirhinos To 4 ft. (1.2 m)
Thick snake has an upturned snout.

Ringneck Snake
Diadophis punctatus To 30 in. (75 cm)
Dark snake has a neck ring and yellow to red belly scales.

Black Racer
Coluber constrictor
To 6 ft. (1.8 m)

Red-bellied Snake
Storeria occipitomaculata
To 16 in. (40 cm)
Brown to black snake has a light collar formed by 3 spots.

Northern Water Snake
Nerodia sipedon To 4.5 ft. (1.4 m)
Note dark blotches on back.

Milk Snake
Lampropeltis triangulum
To 7 ft. (2.1 m)

Massasauga
Sistrurus catenatus To 40 in. (1 m)
Rattlesnake is Ontario's only venomous species.

Brown Snake
Storeria dekayi To 20 in. (50 cm)
Has 2 rows of dark spots down its back.

REPTILES & AMPHIBIANS

Mudpuppy
Necturus maculosus To 16 in. (40 cm)
Told by feathery, reddish external gills.

Eastern Newt
Notophthalmus viridescens
To 6 in. (15 cm)
Immature land form called an "eft" is red orange.

Four-toed Salamander
Hemidactylium scutatum
To 4 in. (10 cm)
Red-brown above, white and black-spotted below.

Long-toed Salamander
Ambystoma macrodactylum
To 7 in. (18 cm)
Has line of light blotches down back.

Tiger Salamander
Ambystoma tigrinum
To 13 in. (33 cm)
Pattern of yellowish and dark blotches is variable.

Bullfrog
Lithobates catesbeianus
To 8 in. (20 cm)
Call is a deep-pitched – *jug-o-rum*.

Pickerel Frog
Lithobates palustris
To 3.5 in. (9 cm)
Call is a snore-like croak lasting up to 3 seconds.

Northern Leopard Frog
Lithobates pipiens
To 4 in. (10 cm)
Brown to green frog has dark spots on its back. Call is a rattling snore.

Wood Frog
Lithobates sylvaticus
To 3 in. (8 cm)
Note dark mask. Staccato call is duck-like.

Mink Frog
Rana septentrionalis
To 3 in. (8 cm)
Call is a metallic – *kuk-kuk-kuk*.

Woodhouse's Toad
Anaxyrus woodhousii
To 5 in. (13 cm)
Call is a sheep-like bleating.

Chorus Frog
Pseudacris triseriata
To 1.5 in. (4 cm)
Note dark stripes on back. Call sounds like running a thumbnail over the teeth of a comb.

American Toad
Anaxyrus americanus
To 4.5 in. (11 cm)
Call is a high musical trill lasting up to 30 seconds.

Spring Peeper
Pseudacris crucifer To 1.5 in. (4 cm)
Note dark X on back. Musical call is a series of short peeps.

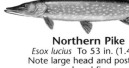

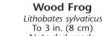

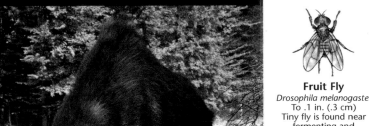

BIRDS

Common Loon
Gavia immer To 3 ft. (90 cm)
Haunting call sounds like –
yodel-ha-oo-oo.
Winter / Summer

Pied-billed Grebe
Podilymbus podiceps
To 13 in. (33 cm)
Note banded white bill.

Blue-winged Teal
Spatula discors To 16 in. (40 cm)

Mallard
Anas platyrhynchos To 28 in. (70 cm)

Northern Pintail
Anas acuta To 30 in. (75 cm)

American Black Duck
Anas rubripes To 25 in. (63 cm)

American Wigeon
Mareca americana To 23 in. (58 cm)

Common Goldeneye
Bucephala clangula To 18 in. (45 cm)

American Coot
Fulica americana To 16 in. (40 cm)

Canada Goose
Branta canadensis
To 45 in. (1.14 m)

Common Merganser
Mergus merganser
To 27 in. (68 cm)
Note slender profile
and thin red bill.

Virginia Rail
Rallus limicola
To 9 in. (23 cm)

**Black-crowned
Night-Heron**
Nycticorax nycticorax
To 28 in. (70 cm)

**American
Woodcock**
Scolopax minor
To 12 in. (30 cm)
Chunky, long-billed bird.

BIRDS

Great Blue Heron
Ardea herodias
To 4.5 ft. (1.4 m)

**Spotted
Sandpiper**
Actitis macularius
To 8 in. (20 cm)
Breast is spotted.

Sanderling
Calidris alba To 8 in. (20 cm)
Runs in and out with
waves along shorelines.

Killdeer
Charadrius vociferus
To 12 in. (30 cm)
Note two breast bands.

Herring Gull
Larus argentatus
To 26 in. (65 cm)
Legs are pinkish.

Ring-billed Gull
Larus delawarensis
To 20 in. (50 cm)
Bill has dark ring.

**Double-crested
Cormorant**
Phalacrocorax auritus
To 3 ft. (90 cm)

Belted Kingfisher
Megaceryle alcyon
To 14 in. (35 cm)

**Mourning
Dove**
Zenaida macroura
To 13 in. (33 cm)

**American
Kestrel**
Falco sparverius
To 12 in. (30 cm)

Rock Pigeon
Columba livia
To 13 in. (33 cm)

Bald Eagle
*Haliaeetus
leucocephalus*
To 40 in. (1 m)

Red-tailed Hawk
Buteo jamaicensis
To 25 in. (63 cm)

**Northern
Flicker**
Colaptes auratus
To 13 in. (33 cm)
Wing and tail
linings are yellow.

**Great
Horned Owl**
Bubo virginianus
To 25 in. (63 cm)
Call is a resonant –
hoo-HOO-hoooo.

BIRDS

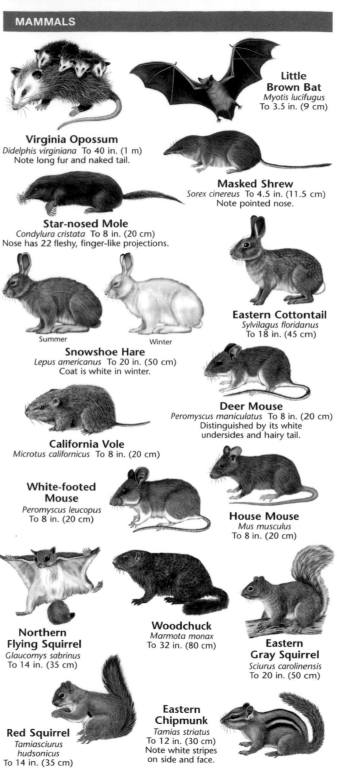
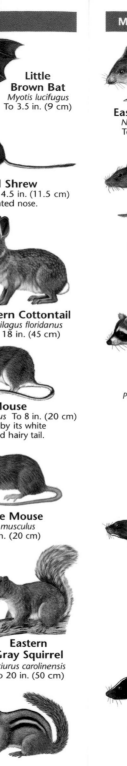

**Ruby-throated
Hummingbird**
Archilochus colubris
To 3.5 in. (9 cm)

Blue Jay
Cyanocitta cristata
To 14 in. (35 cm)

**Common
Nighthawk**
Chordeiles minor
To 10 in. (25 cm)
Often hawks for
insects around
street lights.

**Ring-necked
Pheasant**
Phasianus colchicus
To 3 ft. (90 cm)

**Red-winged
Blackbird**
Agelaius phoeniceus
To 9 in. (23 cm)

European Starling
Sturnus vulgaris
To 8 in. (20 cm)

Barn Swallow
Hirundo rustica
To 8 in. (20 cm)
Note deeply
forked tail.

American Crow
Corvus brachyrhynchos
To 22 in. (55 cm)
Call is a distinct – caw.

Purple Martin
Progne subis
To 8 in. (20 cm)

American Robin
Turdus migratorius
To 11 in. (28 cm)

**American
Goldfinch**
Spinus tristis
To 5 in. (13 cm)

**House
Sparrow**
Passer domesticus
To 6 in. (15 cm)

Dark-eyed Junco
Junco hyemalis
To 7 in. (18 cm)
'Slate-colored'
Race

Yellow Warbler
Setophaga petechia
To 5 in. (13 cm)

House Finch
Haemorhous mexicanus
To 6 in. (15 cm)

Northern Cardinal
Cardinalis cardinalis
To 9 in. (23 cm)

MAMMALS

Virginia Opossum
Didelphis virginiana To 40 in. (1 m)
Note long fur and naked tail.

**Little
Brown Bat**
Myotis lucifugus
To 3.5 in. (9 cm)

Masked Shrew
Sorex cinereus To 4.5 in. (11.5 cm)
Note pointed nose.

Star-nosed Mole
Condylura cristata To 8 in. (20 cm)
Nose has 22 fleshy, finger-like projections.

Snowshoe Hare
Lepus americanus To 20 in. (50 cm)
Coat is white in winter.
Summer / Winter

Eastern Cottontail
Sylvilagus floridanus
To 18 in. (45 cm)

Deer Mouse
Peromyscus maniculatus To 8 in. (20 cm)
Distinguished by its white
undersides and hairy tail.

California Vole
Microtus californicus To 8 in. (20 cm)

**White-footed
Mouse**
Peromyscus leucopus
To 8 in. (20 cm)

House Mouse
Mus musculus
To 8 in. (20 cm)

**Northern
Flying Squirrel**
Glaucomys sabrinus
To 14 in. (35 cm)

Woodchuck
Marmota monax
To 32 in. (80 cm)

**Eastern
Gray Squirrel**
Sciurus carolinensis
To 20 in. (50 cm)

Red Squirrel
*Tamiasciurus
hudsonicus*
To 14 in. (35 cm)

**Eastern
Chipmunk**
Tamias striatus
To 12 in. (30 cm)
Note white stripes
on side and face.

MAMMALS

Eastern Woodrat
Neotoma floridana
To 16 in. (40 cm)

Muskrat
Ondatra zibethicus
To 2 ft. (60 cm)
Aquatic rodent has
a naked tail that
is flattened on
its sides.

Norway Rat
Rattus norvegicus
To 18 in. (45 cm)
Brown to gray
rodent has
a naked tail.

**Common
Porcupine**
Erethizon dorsatum
To 3 ft. (90 cm)
Large rodent has
barbed quills near
its rear that it
uses for defense.

American Badger
Taxidea taxus
To 35 in. (88 cm)

Common Raccoon
Procyon lotor To 40 in. (1 m)

American Beaver
Castor canadensis
To 4 ft. (1.2 m)
Has flat, paddle-like tail.

American Marten
Martes americana
To 26 in. (65 cm)

**Northern
River Otter**
Lontra canadensis
To 52 in. (1.3 m)

Mink
Neovison vison
To 28 in. (70 cm)
Chin is white.

Long-tailed Weasel
Mustela frenata To 21 in. (53 cm)
Note brown feet and
yellowish neck.

Striped Skunk
Mephitis mephitis
To 32 in. (80 cm)

Short-tailed Weasel
Mustela erminea To 14 in. (35 cm)
Note white feet. Coat may turn
white in winter. Also known as ermine.

MAMMALS

Gray Wolf
Canis lupus To 6.5 ft. (2 m)
Coat color is usually gray, but black,
white and mottled variants exist.

Red Fox
Vulpes vulpes To 40 in. (1 m)
Note white-tipped tail.

Common Gray Fox
Urocyon cinereoargenteus
To 3.5 ft. (1.1 m)
Note black-tipped tail.

Lynx
Lynx lynx To 42 in. (1.06 m)

Bobcat
Lynx rufus To 4 ft. (1.2 m)
Has dark lines on top
of its "bobbed" tail.

Coyote
Canis latrans
To 52 in. (1.3 m)
Note bushy,
black-tipped tail.

White-tailed Deer
Odocoileus virginianus To 7 ft. (2.1 m)
Holds flag-like tail aloft while running.

Caribou
Rangifer tarandus To 8 ft. (2.4 m)

Black Bear
Ursus americanus To 6 ft. (1.8 m)

Moose
Alces alces To 10 ft. (3 m)